HAZARDOUS WASTE SITES

Kathiann M. Kowalski

LERNER PUBLICATIONS COMPANY • MINNEAPOLIS

This book is dedicated to my husband, Michael Meissner, who always tries to understand all sides of an issue, and who encourages our children and other young people to become critical and independent thinkers.

Thanks to the many people whose comments and help contributed to this book: Bob Downing of the *Akron Beacon Journal*; Debra Gray at Metcalf & Eddy; Ray Harbisson at the University of Florida; Yvette Harris and Dante Rodriguez at EPA; Becky Hans, Dave Lanzola, Joanne Simanec, and Rick Whartenby at Halliburton NUS Laboratories; Keith Mast and Paul Sanner at Woodward-Clyde Consultants; Ken Moore at Squire, Sanders & Dempsey; Tammy Proctor at the *Hartville News*; David Sharpe at Sharpe & Associates; Philip DeLuca at Sevenson Environmental Services; and Larry Sweeney and Elizabeth Ubinger at Philip Environmental. Thanks also to my resident critics and occasional photographers: Chris, Laura, and Bethany Meissner.

Library of Congress Cataloging-in-Publication Data

Kowalski, Kathiann M., 1955-
    Hazardous waste sites / Kathiann M. Kowalski.
    p. cm. — (Pro/Con)
    Includes bibliographical references and index.
    Summary: Discusses the dangers of hazardous waste sites, who is responsible for the problem, who is responsible for cleanup, various legal decisions, and the effects of the federal Superfund.
    ISBN 0-8225-2609-3 (alk. paper)
    1. Hazardous wastes—United States—Juvenile literature.
    2. Hazardous waste sites—United States—Juvenile literature.
    [1. Hazardous waste sites. 2. Pollution.] I. Title. II. Series
    TD1030.5.K69 1996   95-12687
    363.72'87—dc20

Manufactured in the United States of America
1 2 3 4 5 6 – JR – 01 00 99 98 97 96

CONTENTS

FOREWORD

*If a nation expects to be ignorant and free, . . . it expects what
never was and never will be.*

Thomas Jefferson

Are you ready to participate in forming the policies of our
government? Many issues are very confusing, and it can be difficult to know what to think about them or how to make a decision about them. Sometimes you must gather information about
a subject before you can be informed enough to make a decision. Bernard Baruch, a prosperous American financier and an
advisor to every president from Woodrow Wilson to Dwight D.
Eisenhower, said, "If you can get all the facts, your judgment
can be right; if you don't get all the facts, it can't be right."

But gathering information is only one part of the decision-
making process. The way you interpret information is influenced by the values you have been taught since infancy—ideas
about right and wrong, good and bad. Many of your values are
shaped, or at least influenced, by how and where you grow up,
by your race, sex, and religion, by how much money your family has. What your parents believe, what they read, and what
you read and believe influence your decisions. The values of
friends and teachers also affect what you think.

It's always good to listen to the opinions of people around
you, but you will often confront contradictory points of view
and points of view that are based not on fact, but on myth. John
F. Kennedy, the 35th president of the United States, said, "The
great enemy of the truth is very often not the lie—deliberate,
contrived, and dishonest—but the myth—persistent, persua-
sive, and unrealistic." Eventually you will have to separate fact
from myth and make up your own mind, make your own decisions. Because you are responsible for your decisions, it's im-

portant to get as much information as you can. Then your decisions will be the right ones for you.

Making a fair and informed decision can be an exciting process, a chance to examine new ideas and different points of view. You live in a world that changes quickly and sometimes dramatically—a world that offers the opportunity to explore the ever-changing ground between yourself and others. Instead of forming a single, easy, or popular point of view, you might develop a rich and complex vision that offers new alternatives. Explore the many dimensions of an idea. Find kinship among an extensive range of opinions. Only after you've done this should you try to form your own opinions.

After you have formed an opinion about a particular subject, you may believe it is the only right decision. But some people will disagree with you and challenge your beliefs. They are not trying to antagonize you or put you down. They probably believe that they're right as sincerely as you believe you are. Thomas Macaulay, an English historian and author, wrote, "Men are never so likely to settle a question rightly as when they discuss it freely." In a democracy, the free exchange of ideas is not only encouraged, it's vital. Examining and discussing public issues and understanding opposing ideas are desirable and necessary elements of a free nation's ability to govern itself.

The Pro/Con series is designed to explore and examine different points of view on contemporary issues and to help you develop an understanding and appreciation of them. Most importantly, it will help you form your own opinions and make your own honest, informed decision.

Mary Winget
Series Editor

A solid waste facility in Montgomery County, Maryland

SITES OF CONTROVERSY

He wears a red cape, hood, and gas mask, but Captain Cleanup isn't trick-or-treating. Joined by members of a neighborhood group from Uniontown, Ohio, the costumed character marches to the corporate headquarters of local manufacturers that have sent more than a million gallons of waste to a local landfill. The demonstrators bring black barrels labeled "poison" and "toxic waste" and present "awards" from their "Toxic Hall of Fame."

The landfill, owned by Charles Kittinger and Hyman Budoff, is now closed. The citizens' group, called Concerned Citizens of Lake Township, fears that chemicals could leak from the landfill and pollute air and drinking water. Cancer is their biggest fear, but they worry about other diseases too.

When manufacturers around Akron and Canton, Ohio, sent waste to the landfill more than 20 years ago, they were not breaking any laws. Kittinger and Budoff got licenses from county and state authorities to operate the landfill, and more than 3,000 other individuals and businesses also used it.[1]

A STRANGE CLASSROOM

On May 16, 1988, a group of schoolchildren gathered with their parents and teachers on the steps of the state capitol in Sacramento, California. Calling themselves Mothers Involved in Fighting Toxics, the group claimed that a 250-acre waste disposal facility operated by Casmalia Resources in Casmalia, California, was responsible for birth defects and other illnesses. One girl read from a poem she had written:

> Dear God who watches over me
> Please help me solve this mystery
> They're hurting my family
> They're killing my community
> Oh why God is this government doing this to me?

"This is a long way to go to get to school," said spokesperson Angie Irmiter, "but these kids have a lot to teach our legislators about what it's like to live and go to school next to a toxic waste dump."[2]

CONGRESSIONAL HEARINGS AND COURTROOM BATTLES

Hazardous wastes are chemicals and chemical by-products that can endanger human health or the environment. Each year factories and other sources produce millions of tons of waste. Trying to solve the problem, Congress holds hearings to find out what's causing delays and why cleanup costs are so high.[3]

Arguments about hazardous waste sites rage in the courts, too. Lawyers argue about whether a company should have to pay millions of dollars for cleanup if it did not violate the law when it disposed of the waste.

Residents of Highland Park, Michigan, protest a plan to locate a hazardous medical waste incinerator in their community.

The company insists that its materials are not the cause of environmental problems anyway.[4]

In Riverside County, California, 3,800 people sue more than 200 companies whose waste was dumped at the Stringfellow Acid Pits. The list of defendants includes Montrose Chemical Corporation, Rockwell International, and dozens of other large corporations. The companies say they did nothing wrong.[5] Newspaper reporters follow the debates closely as the arguments rage on.

STILL COUNTING

How many hazardous waste sites are there in the United States? The U.S. Environmental Protection

Cleanup begins at the Stringfellow Acid Pits. A silica gel is injected into the underlying fractured bedrock to seal cracks and fissures.

Agency (EPA), which was established in 1970 to protect the nation's environment from pollution, has estimated there are more than 32,000 places where hazardous substances have been disposed of—either legally or illegally.[6]

Some people fear the government estimate is far too low because the EPA depends upon reports made by the companies that used the waste sites. Also, corporations don't always keep records of waste disposal that took place 20, 30, or even 50 years ago.

Critics like former Washington governor Dixy Lee Ray point out that just knowing the total number of disposal sites does not tell you how many of them are dangerous to people or to the environment.[7] The term hazardous waste is defined broadly and includes many

Each year, factories such as these in Detroit, Michigan, produce millions of tons of waste.

substances found in most homes. According to the Resource Conservation and Recovery Act (RCRA) of 1976 and its 1984 amendments, a substance is considered hazardous if it corrodes (wears away other materials); explodes; is easily ignited; reacts strongly with water; is unstable to heat or shock; or is poisonous. Another word for poisonous is *toxic*.

The EPA publishes a National Priorities List of hazardous waste sites that may require cleanup under federal environmental programs. When this list was first published in 1982, it had just over 400 sites. By 1994 the number had grown to 1,232.[8] How and why did hazardous chemicals get to all these places to begin with? Can all these sites ever be cleaned up?

Although nearly everyone wants a clean environment, cleaning up hazardous waste dumped decades ago would cost billions of dollars. Even then, other social needs compete with environmental goals for funding. Poor people need housing and food. Children need good schools. Cities need roads and bridges. These needs must be balanced with environmental goals.

Companies that own the waste sites and industries that dumped in them care very much about whether there is a cleanup and how that cleanup is carried out. Under federal law, these companies may have to pay millions of dollars for the cleanup. Companies that dumped various kinds and amounts of waste often disagree about what cleanup methods should be used and how much each company should pay.

Federal and state agencies care about hazardous waste sites too. These agencies are responsible for carrying out the laws that protect the environment. They are accountable to the president, Congress, governors, and state legislatures.

What is being done to clean up old hazardous waste sites? What issues are at the center of the debate? What are the positions of government, business, and citizens' groups?

Modern-day shoppers hardly notice the trash awaiting pickup in New York City.

THE WASTE
PROBLEM

Garbage is not a modern invention. Even in prehistoric times, cave dwellers had to dispose of waste. Archaeologists, people who study the artifacts and other remains of early human societies, report finding "kitchen middens," or garbage piles, layered with cooking waste and broken tools and weapons.

When people began to live in cities, methods of waste disposal remained primitive. Often garbage would simply be flung out of houses into narrow streets.[1] Rotting garbage attracts insects and rats that can cause disease. After serious outbreaks of typhoid, cholera, and other diseases in the late 1800s, city dwellers in the United States began to think about waste as a problem. By the 1890s, trash barrels lined the streets of New York City. City workers emptied the barrels periodically and then dumped the waste into the Atlantic Ocean.[2] Many small towns were not even that organized. Until the late 20th century, families in rural areas often had to hire trucking companies to take their waste to an open dump beyond the town limits. Vice President Al Gore once said, "It's practically an American tradition: waste has long been dumped on the cheapest, least desirable land in areas surrounded by less fortunate citizens."[3]

When most dumps began operating, they were "out of sight and out of mind." After World War II (1941–1945), however, many Americans moved to the

This engraving shows the condition of street sanitation in New York in 1875 and the reactions of some passersby.

suburbs. Eventually the suburbs expanded until they came close to some of these dumps. The exposed trash invited various insects and rodents to feast on the waste and then carry disease into the surrounding neighborhoods. Ponds of water dotting the dumps became prime breeding places for disease-carrying mosquitoes. Heavy trucks rumbling toward the landfills sometimes left blowing trash behind them, and loud bulldozers operated from early morning until evening. Since decaying garbage produces heat, fire posed another possible hazard.[4] Something had to be done.

FIRST STEPS TOWARD WASTE MANAGEMENT

In 1965 Congress passed the Solid Waste Disposal Act and also called on the states to adopt laws to regulate solid waste disposal. By 1975, 49 states had adopted such laws. Of the 17,000 reported disposal sites, however, 94 percent still didn't meet minimum requirements.[5]

Incineration, or burning, offered one alternative to the open dump, but the early incinerators were often poorly designed and operated. Besides the danger of fires and explosions, incinerators caused air pollution. Why put up with odors and smoke, people asked, when land disposal was cheaper and safer?[6]

Government officials and sanitary engineers recommended that open dumps be replaced by sanitary landfills. Instead of lying exposed to wind, insects, and rodents, waste would be covered with soil on a daily basis. The soil cover would reduce odors, blowing garbage, and other problems.[7] Sanitary engineers of the 1970s believed that bacteria in the soil would break down the waste, leaving nutrients that could be used by plants.

New sanitary landfills were often built on top of a layer of natural clay, above the groundwater level. Clay is a nonporous substance that helps prevent waste from contaminating surrounding areas. But many older

A garbage truck deposits its load at a sanitary landfill near St. Paul, Minnesota.

This factory stores its chemical waste in drums on its own grounds.

sites continued to operate, even though they didn't meet the new licensing requirements. The owners simply agreed to cover the new waste on a daily basis—thus turning the dump into a sanitary landfill.[8] For a while, sanitary landfills seemed to have solved the waste disposal problem, but eventually people began to worry about what happened to the waste after it was buried.

FOCUS ON HAZARDOUS WASTE

The United States changed from a rural nation into an industrial one within its first 200 years. In the mid-1800s, the Industrial Revolution created an enormous increase in production. As factories manufactured more and more products, the volume of waste grew dramatically too. Where did all this waste go?

If much land surrounded a company's manufacturing plant, the waste might not have gone anywhere. For a long time, industrial waste could legally be dumped onto the "back 40" acres. This practice continued well into the 1900s. Other corporations sent waste to the same dumps and landfills that received household trash. In many cases, state and local laws allowed this practice. The dumps, however, had not been designed to handle chemical waste.

Some businesses sent their chemical waste to special disposal companies that claimed they could discard waste safely. In the early 1970s, Dr. John Miserlis, a chemical engineer and former professor, announced he would recover chemicals from waste at the Silresim Chemical Corporation in Lowell, Massachusetts. Instead, the waste stayed in metal drums stacked 10 feet high on a 5.2-acre site near the River Meadow Brook, which flows into the Concord River. When the drums were exposed to weather, they began to rust and leak.[9]

Seymour Recycling Corporation in Seymour, Indiana, and Summit National Services in Deerfield Township, Ohio, were other sites at which owners failed to

Incinerators like the one above offer one alternative to dumps and landfills.

treat waste as they had promised. The Chem-Dyne Corporation in Hamilton, Ohio, was supposed to send all waste to safe disposal facilities. Instead, operators Bruce Whitten and William Kovacs stockpiled thousands of drums directly on the property.[10]

At Stringfellow Acid Pits in Glen Avon, California, owner J.B. Stringfellow followed instructions from government officials but still wound up dumping chemicals onto the ground.[11] As the situation worsened across the country, ponds of toxic chemicals and grave-yards of filled drums sprouted up from coast to coast.

Environmental groups, such as the Sierra Club and the Environmental Defense Fund, are now appalled by such disposal practices. They claim that the companies

Workers drill 78 wells south of the Stringfellow site to monitor the groundwater.

cared only about keeping disposal costs as low as possible. But 30 or 40 years ago, waste disposal companies didn't realize that environmental problems would result from their practices. Not even the state and local government agencies that licensed landfills knew enough to forbid certain practices, such as pouring hazardous waste onto the ground.

The Resource Conservation and Recovery Act was supposed to provide "cradle-to-grave" regulation of hazardous waste.[12] In November 1980, the EPA issued rules defining hazardous waste under the new act. People who produced and transported hazardous waste had to keep careful records and had to package and transport the waste as specified by law. Businesses (also called TSD facilities) that treated, stored, or disposed of hazardous waste had to get a permit and follow regulations.[13]

Environmental laws have dramatically changed the way industry disposes of its chemical waste. Unfortunately, just about the time the RCRA program began dealing with new hazardous waste, government agencies discovered major problems with some of the country's old hazardous waste sites.

Cleanup efforts begin at Love Canal. Residents had to evacuate the area when chemicals leaked from an old hazardous waste site.

3

THE SUPERFUND
IS BORN

Perhaps the most notorious hazardous waste site in the United States is Love Canal, located near Niagara Falls, New York. More than 70,000 tons of chemical waste were buried in drums stored in the 3,000-foot-long canal from the 1920s through 1953.

When Love Canal was filled to capacity, Hooker Chemical Company, its owner, put a huge clay "cap" over the site to keep rainwater from penetrating the soil and carrying dissolved chemicals to adjacent properties. The nonporous cap was also supposed to keep people from disturbing the buried waste.

In 1953, however, the Niagara Falls school board needed land for a new school and approached Hooker Chemical Company. The company reluctantly sold the property to the local government for one dollar. The deed to the property warned about buried waste and said the chemical company would not be responsible for any health problems or injuries.

Despite the warning, the city decided to build a school over Love Canal. But the construction work

An aerial view of the Love Canal area

broke the clay cap. The buried drums began to rust, and chemicals slowly seeped into the surrounding area.[1]

In 1958 construction workers building a new road near the school discovered chemicals leaking from the drums. Children playing nearby got chemical burns from touching contaminated soil. Local officials had the drums reburied, but that didn't stop the problems. Over the next two decades, some residents got liver disease and others developed chromosome damage. In the 1970s, several parents complained that their children had been born with birth defects.

Who was responsible for the problem at Love Canal? Should the chemical company be blamed for burying its waste, even though it didn't break any law? How

could the company have foreseen that waste would eventually leak out?

Was the local government responsible, since it bought the Love Canal property in spite of the company's warning? Did city officials honestly not realize the seriousness of the problem? And did the chemicals actually make anyone sick? For people living at Love Canal, the answer to the last question was a resounding "yes." When one seven-year-old boy died of a kidney disease that doctors linked to contamination, his mother, Luella Kenny, mourned that "he died of playing in his own backyard."[2]

The chemical company and others disagreed. Dr. Elizabeth Whelan of the American Council of Science and Health conceded that chemicals had leaked from the waste area, but she claimed there was no proof that the chemicals had actually made anyone sick.[3] Nevertheless, residents demanded action. They wanted to move, but no one would buy their houses.

Finally, between 1978 and 1980, the federal and state governments bought the area homes—approximately 1,000 of them—and relocated the residents at a cost of more than $15 million.[4] But the problem of what to do about the chemicals buried at Love Canal remained. As people throughout the nation learned about Love Canal, they worried about waste disposal sites in their own neighborhoods. They demanded that Congress take action.

A SUPERFUND FOR CLEANUP

In response to public outcries about hazardous waste sites, Congress passed the Comprehensive Environmental Response, Compensation, and Liability Act in December 1980. Known as CERCLA or the "Superfund," the act set up a massive program to identify and respond to contamination from hazardous waste sites. Congress knew that the cleanup of hazardous waste sites would be expensive—that's where the name *Superfund* came from. The fund first provided $1.6 billion to clean up unsafe dump sites, but Congress increased the amount to $8.5 billion when the Superfund was reauthorized in 1986.

Where does all this money come from? Part of it comes from special taxes on industry.[5] The government can also sue the people or companies responsible for producing and disposing of the hazardous waste. In this way, the government can regain some of the money it spends on cleanup.

TARGETING SITES FOR CLEANUP

Besides setting up a cleanup fund, the Superfund bill called for the people who owned or operated hazardous waste sites to notify the EPA. Those who produced hazardous waste or hauled waste to a site also had to notify the agency. People were also required to notify the EPA about new chemical spills and other related problems. Failure to give the required notice could mean huge penalties and even possible imprisonment.[6]

The Superfund legislation authorizes the government to take action when there is an actual or threatened release of hazardous substances into the environment. The term *hazardous substance* includes not only hazardous waste but also a variety of chemicals that are regulated under other federal laws.[7]

After the EPA compiled the list of sites where hazardous substances had been disposed, it began preparing a National Priorities List to rank those sites—with the most dangerous sites at the top of the list. People who worry about contamination from a particular site usually want to get it on the National Priorities List, because they feel cleanup will then take place more quickly. On the other hand, companies that have sent hazardous waste to a site may worry that once the site is on the list, cleanup may be costly for them—even if there is no danger to the public or the environment.

When the National Priorities List was first published in 1982, it included 418 sites. But the EPA kept adding to it. By May 31, 1994, the National Priorities List had grown to 1,232 sites, with 54 more sites proposed to be added.[8]

Using the new Superfund program, the EPA and individual states began cleaning up hazardous substance releases across the nation. Government workers removed hazardous substances by emptying them into tanks and drums and then hauling them away. If some contamination remained, the EPA—along with the state involved—began the more difficult process of finding a long-term remedy.

President Jimmy Carter signs the Superfund bill at a ceremony on December 11, 1980.

Environmental engineers drill at the Love Canal site to monitor ground and water conditions.

When the federal and state governments spend money to respond to hazardous substance releases, they want to replenish their cleanup funds. Deciding who should pay the cleanup costs has led to some intense debates.

An abandoned hazardous waste salvage yard in Beardstown, Illinois

WHO PAYS?

Cleaning up a Superfund site usually costs between $27 million and $40 million. Projected costs for some sites, such as the Rocky Mountain Arsenal near Denver, Colorado, exceed $1 billion.[1] At that rate, the Superfund would never be large enough to pay for all the cleanup sites.

To address this problem, Congress included two important provisions in the Superfund program. The "cost recovery" provision states that if the federal government, state government, or even a private citizen spends money to clean up hazardous substances, that party can sue any person or company that is thought to be responsible for causing the pollution.

"Responsible persons" include:

- the present owner or operator of the site;
- the past owner or operator of the site when hazardous substances were disposed there;
- any person who arranged for disposal or treatment of hazardous substances at the site; and
- any person who transported hazardous substances and who selected the site for their treatment or disposal.[2]

Another section of the Superfund program states that the federal government can require "responsible persons" (individuals or companies) to take action themselves if there is an "imminent hazard." The act doesn't explain exactly what an "imminent hazard" is, however. The EPA and companies who are ordered to take action can disagree about whether a site actually presents immediate danger. If a company does not obey an EPA order, the agency can sue for civil (noncriminal) penalties of up to $25,000 per day for each day that the company disobeys the order. If the government then spends its own money for cleanup, a company can also be forced to pay "treble damages"—damages equal to three times the actual cleanup cost.[3]

STRICT AND RETROACTIVE LIABILITY

Businesses got a big shock when the Superfund program was passed. Suddenly they became "strictly liable" for millions of dollars in cleanup costs. In other words, it didn't matter whether they had been careful about disposing of their waste or not.

What made the Superfund program's strict liability, or liability without fault, even more of a shock to industry was that the law applied retroactively. Most laws regulate people's behavior from the time the law is passed. That way, people know what's expected of them. Under Superfund regulations, however, even if a company had disposed of its waste 30 or 40 years ago—when it was lawful to do so—the company must still pay for cleanup.

Advocates of the Superfund's retroactive liability say it provides a logical way to make polluters pay for

An EPA response team monitors emissions from a burning oil spill.

what they have done. Supporters also believe that retroactive liability encourages companies to be careful about how they dispose of new hazardous waste.[4]

Opponents point to the U. S. Constitution's prohibition against *ex post facto* laws that reach back and make conduct unlawful after the fact.[5] They say the Superfund law's retroactive liability is unfair to businesses who obeyed all existing laws when disposal took place. Opponents also say the law's heavy

During a cleanup procedure, geologists must do many soil inspections like this one at the site of the Tex-Tin Corporation in Texas City, Texas.

financial burdens encourage wasteful lawsuits that could be avoided if liability were not retroactive.[6]

JOINT AND SEVERAL LIABILITY

When the Superfund program was first passed, it didn't specify whether a single company could be made to pay all the costs for cleaning up a site—even if many other people's waste contributed to the pollution. The EPA argued that companies should be made to pay for all cleanup costs, not just their own share. In legal terms, this is called *joint and several liability.*

Relying on joint and several liability, the EPA and the Department of Justice have sometimes filed lawsuits against only a few of the parties who sent waste to a site. In *United States v. Conservation Chemical Corporation,* for example, the government sued only 4 of the 300 companies that sent waste to an Indiana disposal facility.[7] In *United States v. Laskin,* the government sued only 8 of the 400 companies that sent waste to the Poplar/Laskin site in Jefferson Township, Ohio.[8]

The companies that are sued in lawsuits like these feel they have been singled out unfairly. Not wanting to bear the burden of cleanup costs themselves, they file claims against other companies that were not named as direct defendants.

The newly named parties (called third-party defendants) also object to being sued. These companies often feel they have a good defense against liability, so they file claims back against the primary defendants and may even bring suppliers, customers, or insurers into the lawsuit. What the government thought would be a straightforward case can turn into a complex lawsuit involving hundreds of companies.

An aerial view of the Poplar/Laskin Superfund site near Jefferson, Ohio

Do you agree with the retroactive "polluter pays" principle, or do you think that companies should not have to pay for cleanup if their actions were lawful at the time the hazardous waste was stored? Is it fair that one company might have to pay all the cleanup costs at a particular site, even if many other companies contributed to the problem? Should Superfund lawsuits include all the companies that sent waste to the site?

CAN WE SETTLE THIS?

Hundreds of lawsuits have been filed under the Superfund program, but only a few cases have gone to trial.

A worker is decontaminated after cleaning up a toxic chemical spill at the McGean-Rohco Company in Livonia, Michigan.

This Iowa landfill is contaminated with arsenic, a highly poisonous element.

The vast majority of Superfund cases are resolved by settlement, or agreement.

Why would people want to settle a Superfund case? For one thing, lawsuits are expensive. Lawyers have to be paid, experts must be hired, and people must take time out from their jobs to testify, locate facts, and do other tasks. Besides, a quick settlement can minimize bad publicity and the possibility of other lawsuits.

The EPA is in the business of protecting the environment rather than filing lawsuits. It prefers that companies agree up front to pay cleanup costs or, when possible, do the work themselves.

Common household supplies often contain hazardous chemicals, although current laws do not apply to the disposal of such products.

MUNICIPAL WASTE

Some Superfund sites took waste only from industries. Many places, however, accepted waste from residences and cities. How does this residential or municipal waste affect debates over cleanup?

FROM OUR OWN GARBAGE CANS

Current laws controlling hazardous waste disposal don't apply to household waste.[1] Still, trash from private homes contains some chemicals that would be called "hazardous" if they came from industry.

Read the labels on products in your home. Look at cleansers, hardware supplies, and automotive products. Check air fresheners and garden supplies. Empty containers and waste from these products often get put in the trash. Or waste gets washed down the drain, where it empties into a septic tank or a wastewater treatment plant. Local authorities must dispose of this waste.

To show just how common hazardous substances are, public health expert Elizabeth Ubinger went shopping at a grocery store, a drugstore, and a hardware store near a hazardous waste site. Then she wheeled a shopping cart into the courtroom.

Sitting in the cart were familiar products, such as dishwashing liquid, decaffeinated coffee, spot remover, furniture polish, rubbing alcohol, mouthwash, windshield washer fluid, motor oil, woodworking glue, brake fluid for cars, and paint thinner. Their ingredients included a host of chemicals: acetone, alcohol, glycol ethers, methylene chloride, trichloroethylene, phenol, naphtha, benzene, ethyl benzene, toluene, xylene, polycyclic aromatic hydrocarbons, hexane, heptane, and tetrachloroethylene. These chemicals can have harmful health effects. Some are even suspected of causing cancer or birth defects.

"As you can see," Ubinger testified, "plenty of things in our home contain all kinds of chemicals." Indeed, many of those substances were the same kinds of chemicals that industrial companies had sent to the nearby hazardous waste site.[2]

IS HOUSEHOLD WASTE REALLY A PROBLEM?
How much of the residential trash hauled to landfills is hazardous waste? Estimates vary from about .5 percent to more than 2 percent.[3] The percentage is small, but .5 percent of a million tons of trash amounts to 10 million pounds of hazardous chemicals.[4]

Cities and other local governments can be liable for cleanup costs of residential waste if they own—or used to own—a landfill in which hazardous waste was disposed. As of 1991, about 14 percent of all the sites on the National Priorities List were municipal disposal sites. That's almost one out of every six sites.[5]

Many local governments do not believe that residential trash creates a significant disposal problem.

If the owner of a Superfund site had mixed hazardous industrial waste with nonhazardous residential waste, a much larger area would have been contaminated. That means cleanup would cost more. For example, at the 190-acre Operating Industries site in Los Angeles, if industrial waste hadn't been mixed with residential waste, cleanup costs would have been much lower than the estimated $600 million.[6]

As household trash decays, it generates methane, an explosive gas made up of carbon and hydrogen. If this

This alley in Detroit, Michigan, has become a dump for old tires.

gas isn't vented properly, it can travel through soil into basements, where it might explode.[7] Also, the congressional Office of Technology Assessment notes that some scientists think methane speeds up the release of other toxic chemicals in hazardous waste sites.[8]

Many local governments and citizens' groups don't believe municipal waste is a significant problem. Critics like writers Rena Steinzor and David Kolker resent the implication that local governments "should pay as much to clean up a garbage bag of twigs and pizza boxes as large corporations must pay to clean up the same amount of toxic chemicals."[9]

The EPA agrees that industrial waste is more to blame than municipal waste for environmental problems. "Nobody at EPA is after the pizza-parlor guy who may have sent his waste to a municipal landfill," said

Bulldozers level the trash and pack it down at Fresh Kills Landfill near New York City.

EPA administrator Carol Browner. "That's not what Superfund is all about."[10]

On the other hand, the EPA has sued owners of municipal landfills. When this has happened, financially strapped local governments have strongly objected to being treated like polluters. Leaders of Woodstock, Illinois, were both surprised and frustrated when their city's 35-acre sanitary landfill was named as a Superfund site. Cleanup costs were estimated to range from $15 million to $25 million.[11]

Community leaders were surprised when this Woodstock, Illinois, landfill was declared a Superfund site.

Amendments to the Superfund program are expected to address the question of municipal waste and liability. The EPA has recommended limiting the liability of people who produced or transported municipal solid waste to as little as 10 percent of total costs.[12] The Superfund would pay the balance.

Do you think that the federal government should help pay for the cleanup of municipal waste? How would you determine what percentage of a site's environmental problems was due to industrial waste rather than municipal trash? Is there a fair way to deal with the issue?

Liquid wastes can be seen in the evaporation ponds at the Stringfellow site in Glen Avon, California.

WHAT IS THE PROBLEM?

Over the course of two decades, J. B. Stringfellow dumped liquid waste from hundreds of companies onto his disposal site in Glen Avon, California. Years later, scientists found an area of contaminated groundwater that ran southward from the disposal site into residential neighborhoods.[1]

Nearly 3,000 miles away from the Stringfellow site is the Lipari Landfill—a 44-acre site near Pitman, New Jersey. The former sand and gravel pit held tons of municipal waste. In addition, owner Nick Lipari took nearly three million gallons of liquid industrial waste from companies such as Owens-Illinois, Almo (a division of Owens-Corning Fiberglass), and Rohm and Haas. The solvents—paint thinners, paints, formaldehyde, dust-collector residues, resins, and phenol and amine waste—contained known and suspected carcinogens—chemicals that have the potential to cause cancer. Waste seeped from the landfill boundaries into soil and groundwater and flowed into Alcyon Lake.[2]

LOCATION OF THE STRINGFELLOW WASTE DISPOSAL SITE

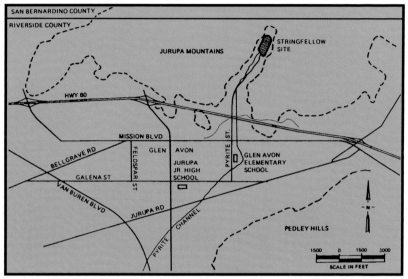

Bedrock underlies the 17-acre Stringfellow disposal site. When the site was chosen, scientists thought the bedrock would prevent any leakage of hazardous waste to the town of Glen Avon. In 1982, however, the site was declared California's highest priority toxic waste site.

Although cleanup work has been going on for more than 12 years—and still continues—the Stringfellow and Lipari Landfill sites are not yet "clean." Indeed, five out of six National Priorities List sites are still contaminated, despite years of work.[3]

PATHWAYS OF EXPOSURE
Chemicals can be dangerous when people, plants, and animals come into contact with them. Chemicals leak from disposal sites through "pathways of exposure."

Water helps chemicals disperse. Liquid waste leaks out of rusted metal drums and tanks. Rainwater dissolves buried chemicals. Flowing downward through the soil, polluted liquids may reach an aquifer—an underground water supply.

Aquifers supply drinking water for almost 50 percent of all people in the United States. That figure includes nearly one-third of the nation's largest cities. In rural areas, about 97 percent of the people use groundwater for drinking and irrigation.[4]

ACT IMMEDIATELY—AND THEN WHAT?

The Superfund program lets the government act immediately to remove hazardous substances that have gotten into the environment. The government can also act

Stringfellow personnel first noticed problems at the site when they saw discolored soil. In 1969, a major storm caused the waste ponds to overflow. Waste materials mixed with rainwater flowed through Glen Avon, several miles downstream from the site.

if there is a threatened release of hazardous substances. Rusting drums, for example, can be taken away to a proper disposal site. Large tanks can be drained as can lagoons holding chemicals.[5]

The EPA can also take other actions when there is an emergency. It can fence a site to keep people away. It can provide bottled water to neighbors, or it can even evacuate people if an immediate health threat occurs. But once emergency action is taken, what happens next? Why does it take years to find a long-term remedy for most hazardous waste sites?

STUDY, STUDY, STUDY

Cleanup takes a long time, sometimes many years, because the law requires that sites be studied and analyzed by experts before long-term cleanup begins. Just how much study is needed before choosing a cleanup plan? If early reports suggest that chemicals have not gotten into water supplies, companies are relieved, because expensive cleanup may not be needed. Residents of the affected area are also relieved to find out that their water has not been poisoned by hazardous chemicals.

Other residents, however, may say that the EPA has not tested thoroughly enough to find contaminants. "There just haven't been enough tests," complained waste site neighbor Terry Witsaman when the EPA announced that fieldwork for its studies at an Ohio site was ending. "You're determining our future based on circumstantial evidence . . . and that's not right and that's not enough."[6]

On the other hand, if the EPA is about to require an expensive cleanup because of early sampling results,

Workers built a system of drainage channels and installed three on-site extraction wells to prevent migration of contaminated groundwater.

companies may want the agency to investigate other possible sources of pollution. Or they may ask the EPA to consider less expensive remedies. At the same time, local residents may worry that the government's plan won't adequately solve the problem. Even if government workers study a site for years, disagreement and distrust often remain among the concerned parties.[7]

"This whole science thing is political," complained Penny Newman, a leader of the California group Concerned Neighbors in Action. "Even if it was scientifically possible to conduct a study here that would show the effect the dump had on our health, they would design it to not show anything."[8]

To add to the confusion, government doesn't speak with one voice. In addition to the EPA, state and local governments are involved in the decision-making process, and each has its own perspective on cleanup.

Contaminated groundwater is extracted from on-site wells like this one. The water contains metals and both organic and inorganic compounds.

Many companies complain that too much study drives up costs. At the same time, industry is cast as the "bad guy" responsible for pollution. As William G. Simeral, former president of the Chemical Manufacturers Association, put it:

> Abandoned dump sites are the single, most obvious symbol of everything the public believes to be wrong with the chemical industry. Whatever their impact on the environment, rusted drums are poisoning the climate for the chemical industry in

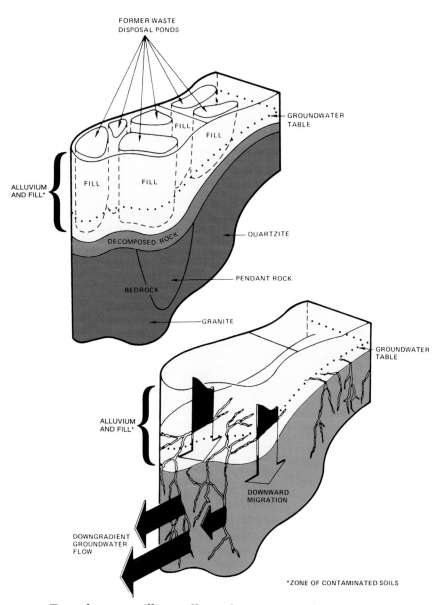

Top, *about 12 million gallons of contaminated groundwater are present in the on-site alluvium and fill layer. Another 4 million gallons are in the decomposed granite, and as much as 6 million gallons are in a section of metamorphic "pendant" rock. The total present in the underlying bedrock is unknown. Bottom, contaminated groundwater is a more significant problem than contaminated soil because water flows from the site to nearby communities.*

Washington and across the nation. As long as we
let the problem persist, we don't stand a chance at
winning the confidence of the people. Individual
companies must get involved—literally—in the
cleanup.[9]

Frustration about continued delays led General Elec-
tric and other companies to support the formation of
Clean Sites, Inc. Founded in 1984, Clean Sites is a non-
profit organization with headquarters in Alexandria,
Virginia. Funded by government and foundation
grants, private gifts, and payment for services, Clean
Sites is dedicated to solving hazardous waste problems
and advancing environmental goals.[10]

PLANS TO SPEED THINGS UP

State agencies and local governments are also involved in the cleanup process. Layers of government
and multiple—often conflicting—viewpoints are involved in deciding whether a problem exists and, if
so, what should be done about it. The EPA has re-
cently begun using its Superfund Accelerated Cleanup
Model (SACM) to speed up studies and decide on
remedies more quickly. Other reforms on the horizon
include use of "generic" remedies for sites with common features.[11]

Will the reforms eliminate criticism about the
agency's study process? There may be fewer delays, but
each site seems special when your company has to pay
for cleanup or when your home is next door to a waste
site. Companies and local citizens are likely to continue arguing that site-specific features mean that either too much or too little study is being done.

Well drilling allows scientists to determine groundwater flow rates and patterns.

Cleanup Option	Capital Cost	Operation and Maintenance Cost	Years of Operation and Maintenance	Present Worth (10%)
• Extract contaminated groundwater • No treatment • SARI line disposal	$6.8 million	$8.4 million	23	$145.6 million
• Extract contaminated groundwater • Granular activated carbon treatment • Reverse osmosis treatment • Reinjection into the aquifer	$15.6 million	$8.9 million	10	$91.6 million
DHS/EPA Proposed Plan • Extract contaminated groundwater • Air stripping treatment • Reverse osmosis treatment • Reinjection into the aquifer	$14.6 million	$7.3 million	10	$76.9 million

Cost estimates were made following EPA National Contingency Plan guidelines so estimated costs could vary by – 30 to + 50 percent.

This cost comparison lists the different community groundwater cleanup options evaluated by the EPA. The proposed plan is the most cost effective, and it meets Superfund cleanup criteria. (See page 62.)

TOO MANY COOKS?

The EPA and even industry-supported groups like Clean Sites believe that people living near a hazardous waste site and other people who have a stake in the outcome should have the opportunity to get involved early in the process. As the Superfund program continues, public participation is likely to increase.[12]

As citizen groups and private companies are allowed more input, will cleanups take even longer?

A respiratory filter and protective gear keep this scientist safe from the contaminated soil and air surrounding him.

HOW CLEAN IS CLEAN?

The National Contingency Plan is a set of federal rules adopted under the Superfund program. Some of the cleanup factors that must be considered include:

- Effectiveness
- Long-term reliability
- Risk to the community
- Community acceptance
- Reasonable cost [1]

These goals often compete with each other. For example, a remedy that seals waste in place may be a cost-effective way to reduce the risk of spreading pollution. The seal would cut off pathways of exposure to toxic chemicals. On the other hand, leaving the waste buried may be unacceptable if people living near the buried waste continue to worry about its long-term effects.

PICK A NUMBER
How clean is clean? In their manual on hazardous waste site cleanups, O'Brien & Gere Engineers claim

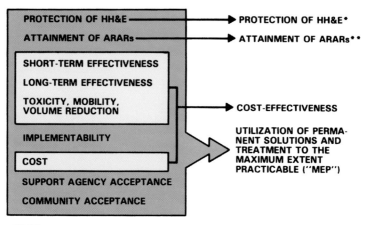

Superfund cleanup criteria must be effective and reliable in both the short term and long term.

that "it is a common misconception that chemicals are inherently dangerous at any level and that hazardous waste sites are a major health threat." Instead, they say, a risk assessment study should "identify the level at which the effects of a hazardous waste site become acceptable to current and future human and animal populations."[2]

A risk assessment looks at the chemicals present at a site, the pathways that could expose people to those chemicals, and the dose at which the chemicals would be harmful. The study can also provide a target goal geared to an "acceptable risk," such as one chance in a million that chemicals remaining on-site would cause an additional case of cancer.[3] At the same time, scientists have learned that even very small doses of certain chemicals might cause cancer, brain damage, or other diseases if a person is exposed to them over a long period of time. Some environmental advocates, such as Ralph Nader at the Public Interest Research Group,

Elizabeth Whelan, of the American Council on Science and Health

claim that chemicals are slowly poisoning America.[4]

Others, like Elizabeth Whelan of the American Council on Science and Health and Nicolas S. Martin at the Consumer Health Education Council, warn against overreacting to reports about trace amounts of chemicals. They argue that many chemicals exist in the general environment at levels that exceed the small amounts that may come from a waste site. Poor diet, lack of exercise, smoking, and alcohol present far greater risks than exposure to chemicals, they say.[5]

Eventually, the EPA is likely to adopt standard cleanup levels for various chemicals. Setting basic standards will make it easier to decide what method should be used to clean up particular waste sites. No matter what method is used or what cleanup standards are set, everybody has an opinion about what a cleanup should accomplish and what the standard for a clean site should be.

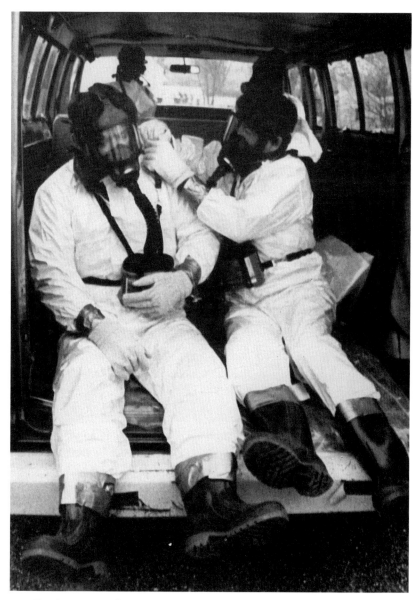

Environmental Protection Agency workers get suited up to retake soil samples in this St. Louis, Missouri, suburb. Dioxin levels were 20 times the maximum safe level.

ENOUGH—OR TOO MUCH?

When the Meramec River flooded in December 1982, about 2,200 people evacuated their homes in Times Beach, Missouri. Once the water level was back to normal, a new threat prevented them from returning home. Soil samples showed that dioxin levels were 20 parts per billion. While this was a tiny amount—equal to about one ounce in eight million gallons of water—it was still 20 times the maximum safe level determined by the Centers for Disease Control in Atlanta, Georgia. Some dioxin compounds are believed to be toxic in concentrations as small as one part per billion.[1]

How had dioxin spread throughout Times Beach? Years before, a man named Russell Bliss worked as an oil scavenger, someone who collects used oil from businesses. Bliss sprayed the oil on roads to keep dust levels down during the summer. Because the waste oil he picked up from Northeastern Pharmaceutical and Chemical Company in Verona, Missouri, contained some dioxin, Bliss had unknowingly spread dioxin over the roads of Times Beach.[2]

Using its authority under the Superfund program, the government relocated almost everyone who lived in Times Beach—at a cost of millions of dollars. Residents were relieved to get away. Less than a decade later, however, Dr. Vernon Houk, the official who had ordered the evacuation, said the move had been an overreaction. He said, "Given what we know about this chemical's toxicity and its effects on human health, it looks as though the evacuation was unnecessary."[3]

Elizabeth Whelan lamented that "decisions and subsequent actions were based on political motivations and not on public health realities."[4]

In 1994 the EPA said the toxicity of the dioxin at Times Beach was as high as ever.

In 1994, however, the EPA released a 2,000-page report concluding that the dioxin's toxicity was as high as ever in Times Beach.[5] People were left wondering just what to believe.

The government felt that if it was going to make a possible error in taking emergency action, it would rather err on the side of protecting human health and the environment. It believed the Times Beach evacuation was the proper action to take. "It was based on the best scientific information we had at the time," said Dr. Houk.[6]

RETURN TO LOVE CANAL

Between 1978 and 1980, federal and state agencies evacuated thousands of people from areas around the Love Canal hazardous waste site. By 1990, however, the EPA said the area was again safe to live in and changed the name of the area to Black Creek Village. "A child runs far, far greater health risks if his parents smoke or drink than he does living in Love Canal," announced James Carr of the Love Canal Area Revitalization Agency.[7]

Had all hazardous waste been removed from Love Canal? The federal government had spent more than $250 million for cleanup over a 12-year period. A state-of-the-art system was built to seal off chemicals in the 16-acre dump, but the chemicals had not been removed. A plastic and clay cap resealed the surface, and monitoring wells surrounded the site to ensure that no chemicals escaped.

Despite government assurances about the safety of the region, the Sierra Club, the Natural Resources

James Carr, director of planning for the Love Canal Area Revitalization Agency, holds a "For Sale" sign as a painter works on a house about to go on the market.

Defense Council (NRDC), and other environmental groups objected. "I'd like to see a lot more information on the health risks before making a major policy decision to move people back," said NRDC attorney Rebecca Todd. "Love Canal is a ticking time bomb."[8]

How did home buyers feel? In 1994 sales agent Kenneth Denman found 33 people waiting in line when he opened his office one Sunday. Only about 100 of the 250 homes in the area were still available. "Love Canal, it seems, is becoming quite a seller's market," he said.[9]

Even after a site has been cleaned up, it can remain a matter of controversy. Most sites are reviewed on a regular basis to see whether any new dangers, such as a new release of chemicals, have developed. New scientific studies might show that a cleanup level previously thought to be acceptable actually involves risks that were never before recognized.

Barrels containing hazardous chemicals are stored beside a residential area in Detroit, Michigan.

DO HAZARDOUS WASTE SITES MAKE PEOPLE SICK?

After Vera sees her children off to school, it's all she can do to clean the kitchen and feed Wiggles, the family's pet rabbit. She feels tired and worn out almost all the time. Vera's worried, too. Her husband, Charles, is having stomach cramps again, and he'll have to go back to the hospital for more tests. Vera and Charles aren't even 45 years old. Could their problems have something to do with the nearby hazardous waste site?

Harvey's had headaches off and on for years. He also gets dizzy spells. Maybe it's just old age. Then again, Harvey wonders if his problems could be caused by chemicals from the closed dump in the area.

Evelyn can't work any more. She's sick and needs an oxygen tank most of the time. Her family doctor can't say what caused her illness, but Evelyn thinks it might be the landfill near her home.

The characters in these examples are made up, but their stories are like those of real people who became

A worker extracts a water sample from the underground water table in Casmalia, California, where a hazardous waste site is located.

sick while living near hazardous waste sites.[1] These people wonder whether their illnesses happened naturally, or whether they were caused by toxic chemicals.

Sometimes residents living near a dump site have similar complaints. Sore throats, headaches, nausea, fatigue, and breathing problems were so common in one California town that a doctor called the illness the "Casmalia Syndrome," after the name of a nearby disposal site.[2]

At other times the health problems of people living in the same area have varied widely. One woman had a miscarriage. A child was born with brain damage. One man had a breathing problem, while another had an

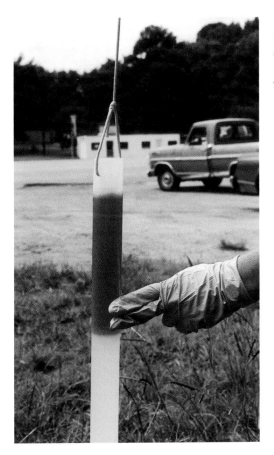

This bailer holds contaminated groundwater from the Kerr-McGee plant in Lakeport, Texas.

irregular heartbeat. Other people complained about headaches and depression. Was it just a coincidence that they all lived near a waste site?

CALL IN THE EXPERTS

How can you tell if hazardous waste caused an illness? Experts like Dr. Bertram Carnow of the University of Illinois School of Public Health and Harvard-trained allergist Dr. Theron Randolph support the claims of

Senator Patrick Moynihan of New York holds a copy of a
government report that states there is not enough evidence
to decide whether it is safe for people to return to Love
Canal.

people who believe that chemicals have made them
sick. The two doctors said that chemicals can harm a
person's ability to fight disease in the same way that
the HIV virus causes AIDS. This view of causation is
sometimes called "chemical AIDS." When residents of
Sedalia, Missouri, complained about health problems
ranging from headaches to kidney infections, Carnow

testified that the ailments were due to a common cause: pollution from a chemical plant owned by Alcolac, Inc.[3]

Other experts, such as Peter Huber of the Manhattan Institute for Policy Research and Elizabeth Whelan, don't believe anyone has proved that waste site chemicals have caused illnesses.

Debate also rages over what dose, or amount, of waste site chemicals causes people to become sick. When scientists do experiments, they usually use animals rather than humans. Professor Bruce Ames at the University of California at Berkeley, who developed one of the leading tests for studying the cancer-causing potential of chemicals, warns that animal studies are often wrongly manipulated to show that chemicals cause cancer in humans. He thinks people are too quick to blame chemicals for many illnesses. Many "natural" substances, such as apples, peanut butter, and coffee, contain chemicals that could be shown to cause cancer in rodents.[4]

WHAT ABOUT OTHER CAUSES?

Former Washington governor Dixy Lee Ray claims that pollution, chemicals in the workplace, industrial products, and food additives cause less than eight percent of all cancer deaths in the United States. "The best scientific evidence points to genetics, viruses, sexual practices, diet, alcohol, and more than anything else, tobacco, as accounting for nearly all of the remaining 92 percent," she says.[5] After studying death rates and causes of disease, Dr. Elizabeth Whelan also concluded that increased use and disposal of industrial chemicals does not coincide with an increase in cancer rates.[6]

Yet these statistics do not impress brothers Ben and Bob Ruzina, who live in Yukon, Pennsylvania. As active members of Concerned Residents of Yough County (CRY), they have campaigned tirelessly to shut down and clean up a nearby hazardous waste site run by Mill Services, Inc. A third Ruzina brother died from cancer. Ben and Bob are convinced that chemicals from the dump caused the disease.[7]

A tank holds hazardous waste at a factory in Dearborn, Michigan.

A bilingual EPA warning sign at the Smith Company in Uvalde, Texas

If you were on the jury in a case claiming that waste site chemicals caused illness, you would listen to testimony from experts on both sides of the issue. Each side would claim it was correct and the other was wrong. How would you decide whom to believe?

This sign opposes the dumping of New Jersey garbage in Barbour County, West Virginia.

10

YOU DECIDE

More than $20.4 billion has been spent so far to clean
up hazardous waste sites. During the first 12 years of
the Superfund program, though, only 180 of the first
1,200 sites on the National Priorities List were offi-
cially "cleaned up."[1] If the rate of cleanup were dou-
bled, it would still take until the year 2030 to address
1,200 sites.

Even if government and private companies move
faster, however, the cleanup for many sites cannot be
completed quickly. Some technologies, such as pump-
ing and treating groundwater, can take decades to
flush out contaminants and reduce pollution to acceptable levels—especially if a large area is involved.
For example, cleanup at the Petro Processors site near
Baton Rouge, Louisiana, is expected to last until the
22nd century.[2]

Meanwhile, the National Priorities List continues to
grow. Some people think as many as 30,000 hazardous
waste sites will eventually need cleanup. Cost estimates for the total cleanup bill range from $27 billion
to almost $2 trillion.[3]

If hazardous waste sites are ignored, will future generations safely be able to enjoy the simple pleasure of a glass of cold water on a hot summer day?

IT'S UP TO YOU

Throughout this book you've been asked what you think and what you would do about hazardous waste sites. These are serious questions. Hazardous waste sites will be around for a long time to come. It will take many years to decide how to clean the sites and who should pay for cleanup costs and personal injuries that may result from hazardous chemicals.

Where will you be in the next 10 or 20 years? By then you may have finished school. You'll probably have a job. Whether you work for a private company or in the public sector (schools, government, police), chances are your place of employment will send materials to a waste site somewhere.

Your company could well be called on to pay cleanup costs for a former hazardous waste site. It could become a defendant in a lawsuit. In any case, it will have to comply with ever-stricter laws for waste disposal. All these developments could have a direct impact on you.

You may even have a family of your own sometime. Where do you think your household waste will go? What will you do if it turns out that your home is within a few miles of a former waste disposal site?

You'll have certain rights and responsibilities in the future. You will vote for leaders to develop and carry out environmental policies. You may even choose to run for office yourself.

The decision is really up to you. What do you think we should do to clean up hazardous waste sites?

Resources to Contact

American Insurance Association
1130 Connecticut Avenue NW
Suite 1000
Washington, DC 20036
202-828-7100

American Petroleum Institute
1220 L Street NW
Washington, DC 20005
202-682-8120

Chemical Manufacturers Association
2501 M Street NW
Washington, DC 20037
202-887-1100

Citizens Clearinghouse for
   Hazardous Waste
P.O. Box 6806
Falls Church, VA 22040
703-237-2249

Clean Sites, Inc.
1199 North Fairfax Street
Suite 400
Alexandria, VA 22314
703-683-8522

Environmental Defense Fund
257 Park Avenue South
New York, NY 10010
212-505-2100

Environmental and Occupational
   Health Sciences Institute
681 Frelinghuysen Road
Piscataway, NJ 08855
908-932-0110

Greenpeace USA
1436 U Street NW
Washington, DC 20009
202-462-1177

Sierra Club
730 Polk Street
San Francisco, CA 94109
415-776-2211

U.S. Environmental Protection
   Agency
401 M Street SW
Washington, DC 20460
202-260-2090

U.S. House of Representatives
The Honorable Congressman or
Congresswoman_____
Washington, DC 20515
202-224-3121

U.S. Senate
The Honorable Senator_____
United States Senate
Washington, DC 20510
202-224-3121

White House
President_____
1600 Pennsylvania Avenue NW
Washington, DC 20500
202-456-1414 or 202-456-1111

Endnotes

CHAPTER 1. SITES OF CONTROVERSY

[1]Bob Downing, "Captain Cleanup to Visit Landfill-Using Firms," *Akron Beacon Journal*, November 1, 1987; "Captain Cleanup Starts Crusade," *Akron Beacon Journal*, November 3, 1987; and telephone conference with Tammy Proctor, *Hartville News*, October 7, 1994.

[2]Fred Setterberg and Lonny Shavelson, *Toxic Nation: The Fight to Save Our Communities from Chemical Contamination* (New York: John Wiley & Sons, Inc., 1993), 34.

[3]U.S. Congress, Office of Technology Assessment, *Are We Cleaning Up? 10 Superfund Case Studies—A Special Report* (Washington, D.C.: Government Printing Office, June 1988); Skip Derra, "OTA Says Superfund Money Is Being Wasted," *Research & Development*, December 1989, 21. See also Michael Kronenwetter, *Managing Toxic Waste* (Englewood Cliffs, N.J.: Julian Messner, 1989), 90–94.

[4]*United States v. Alcan Aluminum Corp.,* 964 F. 2d 252 (3d Cir 1992). See also *United States v. Kramer,* 757 F. Supp. 397 (D.N.J. 1991).

[5]Bruce Van Voorst, "Toxic Dumps: The Lawyer's Money Pit," *Time,* September 13, 1993, 63.

[6]Setterberg and Shavelson, 4; Kathlyn Gay, *Silent Killers: Radon and Other Hazards* (New York: Franklin Watts, 1988), 91.

[7]Dixie Lee Ray and Lou Guzzo, *Environmental Overkill: Whatever Happened to Common Sense?* (Washington, D.C.: Regnery Gateway, 1993), 141–42.

[8]40 C.F.R. Part 300, 59 Fed. Reg. 27989, May 31, 1994. As of May 1994, an additional 54 sites were proposed for addition to the list. Id.

CHAPTER 2. THE WASTE PROBLEM

[1]Martin V. Melosi, *Garbage in the Cities: Refuse, Reform, and the Environment, 1880–1980* (College Station, Texas: Texas A&M University Press, 1981), 4–20; Malcolm E. Weiss, *Toxic Waste: Cleanup or Cover-Up?* (New York: Franklin Watts, 1984), 12–14.

[2]Evan and Janet Hadingham, *Garbage! Where It Comes From, Where It Goes* (New York: Simon & Schuster, Inc., 1990), 8–11. Until the 1930s, the garbage would be loaded onto barges and dumped in the Atlantic Ocean. After trash washed up on New Jersey beaches, the city began using land dumps.

[3]Albert Gore, *Earth in the Balance: Ecology and the Human Spirit* (Boston: Houghton Mifflin Co., 1992), 149.

[4]U.S. Environmental Protection Agency (U.S. EPA), *Your World, My World: A Book for Young Environmentalists* (Washington, D.C.: U.S. Environmental Protection Agency, 1973), 31–33. See also Allen Stenstrup, *Hazardous Waste* (Chicago: Childrens Press, 1991), 75–78; Melosi, 218–20.

[5]Melosi, 200–20.

[6]EPA, *Your World, My World,* 31; See also Hadingham, 30–33; and Homer A. Neal and J.R. Schubel, *Solid Waste Management and the Environment: The Mounting Garbage and Trash Crisis* (Englewood Cliffs, N.J.: Prentice-Hall, 1987), 14–15.

[7]See generally Eugene A. Glysson, James R. Packard, and Cyril H. Barnes, *The Problem of Solid Waste Disposal* (Ann Arbor: University of Michigan College of Engineering Ingenor Series, 1972).

[8]EPA Solid Waste Management Office, *Elements of Solid Waste Management: Training Course Manual* (Cincinnati: EPA, August, 1972).

[9]Michael H. Brown, *Laying Waste: The Poisoning of America by Toxic Chemicals* (New York: Pantheon Books, 1980), 227–28.

[10]See *United States v. Chem-Dyne Corp.,* 572 F. Supp. 802 (N.D. Ohio, 1983); *Ohio v. Georgeoff,* 562 F. Supp. 1300 (N.D. Ohio, 1983); Brown, 228–30.

[11]See *United States v. Stringfellow,* 783 F. 2d 821 (9th Cir 1986). See also Brown, 173–80.

[12]42 U.S.C. §6901 et seq.

[13]40 C.F.R. Part 261 et seq. Hazardous and Solid Waste Amendments of 1984, P.L. 98–616, 98 Stat. 3268, November 8, 1984.

CHAPTER 3. THE SUPERFUND IS BORN

[1]Judith Woodburn, *The Toxic Waste Time Bomb* (Milwaukee: Gareth Stevens Publishing, 1992), 16–20; Lila Gano, *Hazardous Waste* (San Diego: Lucent Books, 1991), 12–20; Brown, 3–59.

[2]Anne Underwood, "The Return to Love Canal," *Newsweek,* July 30, 1990, 25. See also Gano, 14.

[3]Elizabeth M. Whelan, *Toxic Terror: The Truth behind the Cancer Scares* (Buffalo, New York: Prometheus Books, 1993), 123.

[4]See Kronenwetter, 14–15. [The purchase was the first time the Emergency Management Act was used in a case of environmental pollution.] See Stenstrup, 6–13.

[5]For a breakdown of where Superfund Trust Fund money comes from, see Katherine N. Probst and Paul R. Portney, *Assigning Liability for Superfund Cleanups: An Analysis of Policy Options* (Washington, D.C.: Resources for the Future, 1992), 19.

[6]42 U.S.C. §9603.

[7]See 42 U.S.C. §9601(14) for statutory definitions.

[8]40 C.F.R. Part 300, 59 Fed. Reg. 27989, May 31, 1994. For information on the historic growth of the National Priorities List, see Stephen J. Zipko, *Toxic Threat: How Hazardous Substances Poison Our Lives* (Englewood Cliffs, N.J.: Julian Messner, 1986), 127.

CHAPTER 4. WHO PAYS?

[1]Probst and Portney, 17.

[2]42 U.S.C. §9607. Any response actions by a private person must be "consistent with" the National Contingency Plan adopted by EPA, and actions by the federal and state governments must be "not inconsistent with" that plan. The National Contingency Plan is a set of rules that describes how cleanups should be done. It can be found at 40 C.F.R. Part 300.

[3]42 U.S.C. §§9606, 9607(d).

[4] "Make the Polluters Pay,", *USA Today,* September 16, 1994.

[5]U.S. Constitution, Art. I.

[6]Bob Smith, "Stop Unfair Penalties," *USA Today,* September 16, 1994, 12A; Leigh Zimmerman, "Letters to the Editor: Retroactive Penalties Wrong," *USA Today,* September 20, 1994. See also Probst and Portney, 1, 11, 38–39.

[7]*United States v. Conservation Chemical,* 589 F. Supp. 59 (W.D. Mo., 1984). The site owner was also a defendant.

[8]Thomas W. Church and Robert T. Nakamura, *Cleaning Up the Mess: Implementation Strategies in Superfund* (Washington, D.C.: Brookings Institution, 1993), 47–51.

CHAPTER 5. MUNICIPAL WASTE

[1]Hazardous waste disposal is now controlled by Subtitle C of the federal Resource Conservation and Recovery Act.

[2]Colette M. Jenkins, "Is It Moth Balls or Something Worse? Specialist Testifies That Contaminants at Dump Mostly Household Items," *Akron Beacon Journal,* February 11, 1993, 13.

[3]U.S. Congress, Office of Technology Assessment, *Facing America's Trash: What Next for Municipal Solid Waste?* (New York: Van Nostrand Reinhold, 1992), 87; W. L. Rathje, et al., *Characterization of Household Hazardous Waste from Marin County, California, and New Orleans, Louisiana* (Las Vegas: EPA Environmental Monitoring Systems Laboratory, Office of Research and Development, 1987); SCS Engineers, Inc. for EPA, *Survey of Household Hazardous Waste and Related Collection Programs* (Washington, D.C.: EPA, October 1986); Cal Recovery Systems, Inc., *Characterization and Impacts of Nonregulated Hazardous Waste in Municipal Solid Waste of King County* (Seattle: Puget Sound Council of Governments, 1985). See also Stenstrup, 49–61.

[4]Woodburn, 24. One study by Dana Duxbury and Associates of Massachusetts estimated that the average American produces 15 pounds of household hazardous waste each year. Jenny Tesar, *The Waste Crisis* (New York: Facts on File, 1991), 40–41. See also Gay, 113–14.

[5]Cynthia C. Kelly, "Superfund and Local Governments: Making the Process Work," *Public Management,* May 1991, 11.

[6]Ibid.,13; Harold C. Barnett, *Toxic Debts and the Superfund Dilemma* (Chapel Hill, N.C.: University of North Carolina Press, 1994), 263–64.

[7]Kronenwetter, 58; Charlotte Wilcox, *Trash!* (Minneapolis: Carolrhoda Books, 1988), 26.

[8]Office of Technology Assessment, *Facing America's Trash,* 288–89.

[9]Rena I. Steinzor and David Kolker, "Superfund Liability Dumped onto Local Governments," *Government Finance Review,* August 1993, 11.

[10]Van Voorst, 64.

[11]Dennis Anderson, "Woodstock Meets Superfund," *Public Management,* May 1991, 7.

[12]See 103d Congress, HR 3800 and S1834 and reports on those bills, hereafter called "1994 Draft Legislation."

CHAPTER 6. WHAT IS THE PROBLEM?

[1]California Environmental Protection Agency Department of Toxic Substances Control, "Stringfellow Update," August 1994, 3. See *United States v. Stringfellow,* 783 F. 2d 821 (9th Cir 1986); and Brown, 173–80.

[2]See Daniel Mazmanian and David Morell, *Beyond Superfailure: America's Toxics Policy for the 1990s* (Boulder, Colorado: Westview Press, 1992), 57–59.

[3]Van Voorst, 63; Setterberg and Shavelson, 123; Kronenwetter, 87.

[4]Gay, 12, 70–79.

[5]See 42 U.S.C. §9604.

[6]Bob Downing, "Testing Will End At Dump; Neighbors Angry at EPA," *Akron Beacon Journal,* July 13, 1987.

[7]Probst and Portney, 1, 17.

[8]Setterberg and Shavelson, 160.

[9]William G. Simeral and Robert C. Cowen, "The Chemical Industry Is Not Poisoning America," in *The Environmental Crisis: Opposing Viewpoints*, Julie S. Bach and Lynn Hall, eds. (St. Paul: Greenhaven Press, 1986), 180.

[10]Clean Sites, Inc., 1993 Annual Report, 1.

[11]See 1994 Draft Legislation.

[12]See 1994 Draft Legislation. See also Clean Sites, Inc., *A Remedy for Superfund* (Alexandria, Va: Clean Sites, Inc., 1994), 34–42.

CHAPTER 7. HOW CLEAN IS CLEAN?

[1]Statutory and regulatory provisions can be found at Section 121 of the Superfund statute and in the National Contingency Plan, 40 C.F.R., Part 300.

[2]O'Brien & Gere Engineers, Inc., *Hazardous Waste Site Remediation: The Engineer's Perspective* (New York: Van Nostrand Reinhold, 1988), 95.

[3]Ibid., 95–100; Benjamin P. Smith, "Exposure and Risk Assessment," *Hazardous Waste Management Engineering*, ed. Edward J. Martin and James H. Johnson, Jr. (New York: Van Nostrand Reinhold, 1987), 37–79.

[4]Ralph Nader, Ronald Brownstein, and John Richard, "The Chemical Industry Is Poisoning America," 171–176; Lewis Regenstein, "Toxic Wastes Are Causing a Cancer Epidemic," 171–76, 183–88; James Morton, "Environmental Pollution Causes Cancer," 47–53 in *The Environmental Crisis*, Bach and Hall, eds. (St. Paul: Greenhaven Press, 1986).

[5]See generally Whelan, *Toxic Terror;* Nicolas Martin, "Environmental Pollution Does Not Cause Cancer," *The Environmental Crisis*, Neal Bernards, ed. (San Diego: Greenhaven Press, 1991), 54–60.

CHAPTER 8. ENOUGH—OR TOO MUCH?

[1]Weiss, 3–6.

[2]Brown, 230–33.

[3]Keith Schneider, "U.S. Backing Away from Saying Dioxin Is a Deadly Peril," *New York Times*, August 15, 1991.

[4]Whelan, 296. See also Dixy Lee Ray and Lou Guzzo, *Trashing the Planet: How Science Can Help Us Deal with Acid Rain, Depletion of the Ozone, and Nuclear Waste (Among Other Things)* (Washington, D.C.: Regnery Gateway, 1990), 88–90.

[5]Sharon Begley and Mary Hager, "Don't Drink the Dioxin," *Newsweek*, September 19, 1994, 57.

[6]Keith Schneider, "Times Beach Warning: Regrets a Decade Later," *New York Times*, August 15, 1991.

[7]Anne Underwood, "The Return to Love Canal," *Newsweek*, July 30, 1990, 25; See also Verlyn Klinkenborg, "Back to Love Canal: Recycled Homes, Rebuilt Dreams," *Harper's*, March 1991, 71.

[8]Underwood, 25; Gano, 17–18.

[9]Evelyn Nieves, "Loving Love Canal Once More," *New York Times*, July 12, 1994.

CHAPTER 9. DO HAZARDOUS WASTE SITES MAKE PEOPLE SICK?

[1]The names and characters described are fictitious. No resemblance to any real

person is intended, and any such resemblance is purely coincidental.

[2]Peter W. Huber, *Galileo's Revenge: Junk Science in the Courtroom* (New York: Basic Books, 1991), 92–99. See also *Elam v. Alcolac, Inc.,* 765 S.W. 2d 42 (Mo. App. 1988).

[3]Huber, 108–109; Whelan, 19–21.

[4]Bruce N. Ames and Lois Swirsky Gold, "Environmental Pollution and Cancer: Some Misconceptions," in *Phantom Risk: Scientific Inference and the Law,* Kenneth R. Foster, David E. Bernstein, and Peter W. Huber, eds. (Cambridge, Mass.: MIT Press, 1993), 152–81; see also Whelan, 55–60.

[5]Ray and Guzzo, 5.

[6]Whelan, 393–412.

[7]Setterberg and Shavelson, 268–72.

CHAPTER 10. YOU DECIDE.

[1]Van Voorst, 63.

[2]Ibid.

[3]Compare Probst and Portney, 29, noting that the $27 billion estimate for EPA costs is probably low and does not include money paid by private companies; Teser, 47, referencing an Office of Technology Assessment estimate of $100 billion; Van Voorst, 63, suggesting that costs will amount to $1 trillion over the next 50 years; and Church and Nakamura, 3, saying it's unclear whether costs will range to $100 billion or $1.7 trillion.

Glossary

allege: to claim something is true

aquifer: an underground reservoir of water

bedrock: the solid rock underlying surface materials

carcinogen: a chemical that has the potential to cause cancer

chemical AIDS: the name given to a set of symptoms that occur when hazardous chemicals damage the body's ability to fight off disease

Comprehensive Environmental Response, Compensation, and Liability Act (CERCLA): the federal law that set up a program to identify and respond to contamination from hazardous waste sites; also called the Superfund

defendant: someone required to make answer in a legal action or suit.

dioxin: a highly toxic synthetically produced chemical

groundwater: water from underground aquifers or reservoirs

hazardous substance: one of several hundred chemicals that can trigger response action under the Superfund program

hazardous waste: waste that is subject to regulations because of potential hazards in disposing of it

industrial waste: chemicals and other byproducts that result from industrial production

joint and several liability: a defendant's responsibility to pay the entire amount of damages, even if the defendant caused only a part of the harm

landfill: a garbage dump covered with a thin layer of soil

liable: legally responsible

municipal waste: waste from homes, offices, and stores

nonporous: without pores or openings that permit liquids or gases to pass through

remedy: action taken to prevent or minimize the release of hazardous substances on a long-term basis

removal: action taken to prevent or minimize the release of hazardous substances on a short-term basis

Resource Conservation and Recovery Act (RCRA): a federal law controlling the disposal of hazardous waste

response: actions to address hazardous substance releases, including both short-term removals and long-term remedies

retroactive: reaching back in time to include actions that have already taken place

risk assessment: a study to determine the potential risks presented to people from exposure to hazardous chemicals.

sanitary landfill: a disposal site that meets rules for waste disposal, such as the daily covering of waste with soil

settle: to resolve a legal dispute by agreement and without the need for trial. Generally, one party pays money to another in return for the other party giving up his or her legal right to pursue a claim in court.

statute: a law passed by the legislative branch of the government

Superfund: *See* Comprehensive Environmental Response, Compensation, and Liability Act

Bibliography

Bach, Julie S., and Lynn Hall, eds. *The Environmental Crisis: Opposing Viewpoints.* St. Paul: Greenhaven Press, 1986.

Barnett, Harold C. *Toxic Debts and the Superfund Dilemma.* Chapel Hill: University of North Carolina Press, 1994.

Begley, Sharon, and Mary Hager. "Don't Drink the Dioxin." *Newsweek,* September 19, 1994, 57.

Bernards, Neal, ed. *The Environmental Crisis: Opposing Viewpoints.* San Diego: Greenhaven Press, 1991.

Brown, Michael H. *Laying Waste: The Poisoning of America by Toxic Chemicals.* New York: Pantheon Books, 1980.

Church, Thomas W., and Robert T. Nakamura. *Cleaning Up the Mess: Implementation Strategies in Superfund.* Washington, D.C.: Brookings Institution, 1993.

Clean Sites, Inc. *A Remedy for Superfund: Designing a Better Way of Cleaning Up America.* Alexandria, Virginia: Clean Sites, Inc., 1994.

Franck, Irene, and David Brownstone. *The Green Encyclopedia.* New York: Prentice Hall, 1992.

Gano, Lila. *Hazardous Waste.* San Diego: Lucent Books, 1991.

Gay, Kathlyn. *Silent Killers: Radon and Other Hazards.* New York: Franklin Watts, 1988.

Glysson, Eugene A., James R. Packard, and Cyril H. Barnes. *The Problem of Solid Waste Disposal.* Ann Arbor: University of Michigan College of Engineering Ingenor Series, 1972.

Gore, Albert. *Earth in the Balance: Ecology and the Human Spirit.* Boston: Houghton Mifflin, 1992.

Hadingham, Evan, and Janet Hadingham. *Garbage! Where It Comes From, Where It Goes.* New York: Simon & Schuster, 1990.

Huber, Peter. *Galileo's Revenge: Junk Science in the Courtroom.* New York: Basic Books, 1991.

Karlin, Alex S. "How Long Is Clean? The Temporal Dimension to Protecting Human Health under Superfund." *Natural Resources & Environment,* Summer 1994, 6.

Kelly, Cynthia C. "Superfund and Local Governments: Making the Process Work." *Public Management,* May 1991, 11.

Kronenwetter, Michael. *Managing Toxic Waste.* Englewood Cliffs, N.J.: Julian Messner, 1989.

Leggett, Jeremy. *Waste War.* New York & Toronto: Marshall Cavendish, 1991.

Mazmanian, Daniel, and David Morell. *Beyond Superfailure: America's Toxics Policy for the 1990s.* Boulder, Colorado: Westview Press, 1992.

Melosi, Martin V. *Garbage in the Cities: Refuse, Reform, and the Environment, 1880–1980.* College Station, Tex.: Texas A&M University Press, 1981.

Neal, Homer A., and J. R. Schubel. *Solid Waste Management and the Environment: The Mounting Garbage and Trash Crisis.* Englewood Cliffs, N.J.: Prentice-Hall, Inc., 1987.

O'Brien & Gere Engineers, Inc. *Hazardous Waste Site Remediation: The Engineer's Perspective.* New York: Van Nostrand Reinhold, 1988.

O'Connor, Karen. *Garbage.* San Diego: Lucent Books, 1989.

Probst, Katherine N., and Paul R. Portney. *Assigning Liability for Superfund Cleanups: An Analysis of Policy Options.* Washington, D.C.: Resources for the Future, 1992.

Ray, Dixy Lee, and Lou Guzzo. *Environmental Overkill: Whatever Happened to Common Sense?* Washington, D.C.: Regnery Gateway, 1993.

_____. *Trashing the Planet: How Science Can Help Us Deal with Acid Rain, Depletion of the Ozone, and Nuclear Waste (Among Other Things).* Washington, D.C.: Regnery Gateway, 1990.

Setterberg, Fred, and Lonny Shavelson. *Toxic Nation: The Fight to Save Our Communities from Chemical Contamination.* New York: John Wiley & Sons, 1993.

Smith, Benjamin P. "Exposure and Risk Assessment," in *Hazardous Waste Management Engineering.* Edited by Edward J. Martin, and James H. Johnson, Jr. New York: Van Nostrand Reinhold, 1987.

Stenstrup, Allen. *Hazardous Waste.* Chicago: Childrens Press, 1991.

Tesar, Jenny. *The Waste Crisis.* New York: Facts on File, 1991.

Underwood, Anne. "The Return to Love Canal." *Newsweek,* July 30, 1990, 25.

U.S. Congress, Office of Technology Assessment. *Complex Cleanup: The Environmental Legacy of Nuclear Weapons Production.* OTA-O-484. Washington, D.C.: Government Printing Office, February 1991.

_____. *America's Trash: What Next for Municipal Solid Waste?* New York: Van Nostrand Reinhold, 1992.

U.S. Environmental Protection Agency. *Your World, My World: A Book for Young Environmentalists.* Washington, D.C.: U.S. Environmental Protection Agency, 1973.

Van Voorst, Bruce. "Toxic Dumps: The Lawyer's Money Pit." *Time,* September 13, 1993, 63.

Weiss, Malcolm E. *Toxic Waste: Cleanup or Cover-Up?* New York: Franklin Watts, 1984.

Whelan, Elizabeth M. *Toxic Terror: The Truth behind the Cancer Scares.* Buffalo, N.Y.: Prometheus Books, 1993.

Wilcox, Charlotte. *Trash!* Minneapolis: Carolrhoda Books, 1988.

Woodburn, Judith. *The Toxic Waste Time Bomb.* Milwaukee: Gareth Stevens Publishing, 1992.

Zipko, Stephen J. *Toxic Threat: How Hazardous Substances Poison Our Lives.* New York: Julian Messner, 1986.

Index

93

Acknowledgments

American Council on Science and Health, 63; the Bettmann Archive, 16; Jerry Boucher, 18, 43; California Environmental Protection Agency, 10, 22, 48, 50, 51, 53, 54–55, 56 (both), 58, 59, 62; Courtesy: Jimmy Carter Library, 26; Clean Sites, 39; S.C. Delaney/U.S. Environmental Protection Agency, 6; Environmental Response Team, U.S. EPA; 35, 47, 60; Eugene Fisher, 72; Illinois Environmental Protection Agency, 32, 46; Richard B. Levine, 45; National Association of Conservation Districts, cover; Ohio Environmental Protection Agency, Division of Emergency and Remedial Response, 37; Frances M. Roberts, 14; UPI/Bettmann, 24, 27, 28–29, 30, 64, 66, 68, 74; U.S. Environmental Protection Agency, Region 5, 80 (both); United States Environmental Protection Agency, Region 6, 19, 20, 36, 40, 73, 77; Jim West, 8, 11, 13, 38, 44, 70, 76, 78.

95

ABOUT THE
AUTHOR

Kathiann M. Kowalski has seen much controversy in
her 15 years as an attorney practicing environmental
law. She received her bachelor's degree from Hofstra
University in New York and her law degree from
Harvard Law School, where she was an editor of the
Harvard Law Review.

Kowalski is the author of more than a dozen articles
and papers on legal matters, including environmental
law, legal ethics, scientific evidence, and other topics.
She has also written various articles and stories for
children as well as articles on family life.

The author lives in Fairview Park, Ohio, with her
husband and three children.